Incandescent

AHMED ABOELHIBA

Acknowledgements

This book wouldn't have come to fruition without the words of support and encouragement from many of the great friends of mine. My life-long supporter, sister, and friend has a great hand in shaping this book, and so, thank you for everything, Raghad. Present she was in many of the days I wrote these poems on, and she always had to be the first person reading them. It was even her that got me into poetry in the first place.

To Aiza, I always enjoy her profound feedback and constructive critiques on my poems. She aided me when it came to choosing the right words and the right poems that made it to the final cut. With enormous anticipation, she was waiting to see how this project shapes up to be.

To Mel, I am so thankful for her helping me navigate artistic choices for the book's overall design. And to Rein, she has my entire gratitude for illustrating the book and interpreting those words of poetry into art, perfectly inducing the vision of what I wanted this book to be.

To Amanda and Noora, and all my Writing Center friends, they are truly the best. To the times we shared stories together, and to the times we shared some profound conversations, they were all moments that mused me to write more, and they are memories that I will forever hold on to.

No matter how I thank my parents, it would not ever be enough. They made sure opportunities were available for me even if that meant they had to sacrifice their own. Without them, I am not the person I am today, and I would not have been publishing this very book. For them, I am eternally grateful.

To a previous version of myself who never thought I'd make it so far, and to anyone who ever felt or feels the same.

TABLE OF POEMS

CHAPTER I:

Memory Bank

Time's Embrace

The villain I am now,
for pushing away your venom stings
And I am the terrible person,
for choosing the peace my mind brings

How dare I, not put you on a pedestal,
after leaving my heart blooded?
And how could I, choose sleeping carefree,
than with my eyes flooded?

Cannot believe I left the heartache behind,
on to a clean, fresh start
And how rightful are you, expecting me to
endure being ripped apart?

What we once shared in time's embrace
Now into thin air fades, without a trace

A fact it is now, one we have to inevitably accept
A flood of indifference, has you away from
mind swept

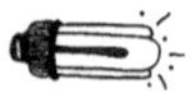

Away They Run

And when they got to know me,
away they have eventually run
Not interesting I might be, or perhaps,
I'm not their type of fun

Shunned I once was by them,
yet it wasn't something in me
It was rather who they have shaped
themselves to be

And it is supposed to hurt, looking around,
and seeing of them, none
Yet I clearly see who they are, with filters,
all undone

And the haze of love that blinded me is now gone
And I have my life cleansed from their presence,
so who really won?

Heartbreak Hotel

Checking in, but I don't want to stay
Just passing through, to get the pain away

Got my bags packed, yet my heart is heavy
Another guest I am, at the heartbreak hotel

It's a lonely place, where the heartache festers
It's a lonely place, where the memory still dwells

Walking down the halls, I hear echoes of my past
Trying to forget, but it's hard to get them
bypassed

A stranger I am here, but the walls know
my name
Nothing helps here, the heartbreak is just
the same

Counting down the hours,
till I can leave this place
Counting down the minutes,
till I forget their face

And until then, just another guest,
I am still here
At the heartbreak hotel, haunted
by the darkest fears

Dim

So hard it is to have good people beside me stay,
So hard it is not to overthink every action I take

I reconsider every possible scenario, and yet,
In each, I do accuse myself of so much guilt

Imperfect is me, them, and literally everyone,
No reason for me to change; neither them too

The light within me dimmed and ultimately
disappeared,
And the memories we shared have me entirely
smeared

Burden

Forever incandescent I thought our spark was,
And not too long till it vanished with no cause

Bored of my presence, eventually they grew
Sick of my character, probably they were too

Saw it coming though, but never this quick
With a soulmate fantasy, I did myself trick

My best I gave not to be a black hole for their light,
Yet, they were nothing but a darkness disguised

Black Holes

But why when I'm the golden light,
the bright soul,
They always end up being one absorbing
black hole

Consequently I isolate and close off myself,
And that's when a pure soul gets me off the shelf

I feel that I'm undeserving of who they are,
That I'm nothing but a burden so bizarre

I force myself into changing and pushing away
the pain,
Maybe I'd wake up being the outgoing soul
once again

Yet when I do, I'm faced with black holes again,
Absorbing everything with no return

And so such cycles continuously restore,
Until the trying isn't worth it anymore

Blind You Were

In front me, about an acquaintance,
you passionately spoke,
How endearing and sweet they were,
you lovingly described

More than a friend, you deeply wished they were,
And astounded you were, by how much they care

Listed traits of someone you wished you so
much knew,
Traits perfectly defining my personality and
who I am

There next to you I was, yet you were blind,
From a soul so precious and said to be kind

Tiny Pebble

Weeks before, slightly frustrated you were,
By how my kind acts had you overwhelmed

Well may be you noticed, yet you still ignored,
The person whom from, you wouldn't get bored

Bored I am now, of your coldness and
indifference,
Of you overlooking my efforts to keep
you around

And when you get to open your eyes and
finally see,
Long lost I will be, as a tiny pebble in the
Pacific sea

Incognito

Anonymous it was, gifts we each other handed,
And the event was, before Christmas arranged

You I didn't know, and me you didn't either.
Yet by luck and fate, my gift you did bring

How happy with it I truly was,
Gifted a book I really wanted

Needed to thank you, but you weren't there,
And told I was, you were traveling somewhere

Then about you and me,
we get to each other know.
We talk, and with each other,
we spend time more

Incognito were the impressions about me
you felt,
With my presence around you being too
frequent

Too much? Annoying?
A burden even?
That about myself I
constantly overthink

A Lot Has Changed Within

From early October to mid-January,
A lot between us has changed within

From hangouts so exciting, to ones you
now barely tolerate,
Forcing them I won't do, and from them
I will you exonerate

A lot between us has changed within,
And the rush dried out soon enough

The ugly contempt was absolutely inevitable,
Though avoiding that, I thought I was capable

Thrilling nights turned to sleepless ones,
Overthinking what could've led us here

Your company truly gave me the best of times,
And my joy has never reached such primes

Did whatever I can unquestionably
to keep you around,
And if I ever time-traveled back,
I'd be doing it once more

From you, I have to move on, though,
No matter how hard it is to do so

Too Good? Misunderstood?

Planning it for you, meticulously,
Was the happiest I could've ever been

Had it from the best place bought,
With a handwritten letter I wrote

So excited I was, handing it you,
Tepidness, in return, was all I got

Was is it my bad being too good?
Or was my gift totally misunderstood?

With it, I wanted nothing but to make your day,
And for you to have a sweet memory in your
mind engraved

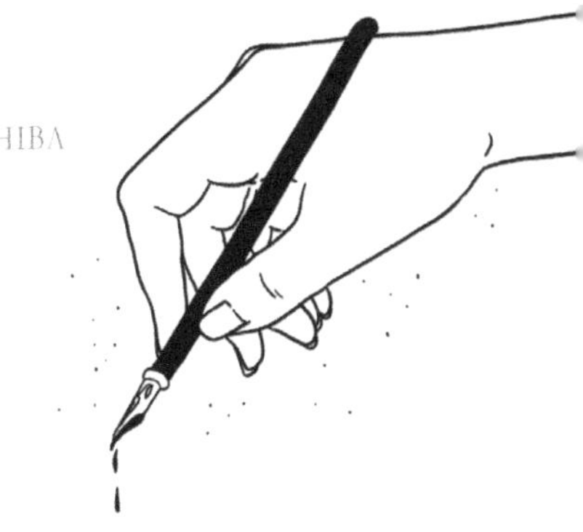

You made my golden
skies so blue,
I now feel guilty being
good to you

Until It's Me

And you can never be more friendly,
With whoever's around, until it's me

You're a listener, so good, so attentive,
Until it's me, that trait is never agentive

In care and compassion you couldn't excel more,
Until it's me, you're too dry of a person yet so cold

Why is that, I don't think I'd ever know.
I'm too good of a person to be treated so

June Xth

It's your birthday, and I quite miss you
Even missing the moments we spent together
having nothing to do

It's your birthday, and I cannot stop thinking
About how close we got and how apart we are
now growing

It's your birthday, and I so much hate you
And I hate how the love I had to you was
very much true

It's your birthday, and I just miss you
And I miss a version of me that've seen you
in a more uplifting view

Deep to The Bone Cut

The first you weren't and nor the last you'd be,
To discard the sweet memories we together had

Never was I so happy than with you around,
Yet from the skies I fell down to the ground

Never have I thought you'd give up on me
in no time
You lost enthusiasm, while I still keep what
I for you had

Never did I enjoy conversations and talks
as much as I did with ours,
And nothing was better than the time we
together spent in bookstores

Expectedly, I knew you wouldn't
forever beside me stay, but,
I did hope your leave of me didn't
as deep to the bone cut

Potential

Feeling something precious is to be finally found,
Yeah, that I first had having them in my life present

Aquatinted long enough to enjoy their company,
And as friends, we evolved so quickly and funnily

And when I thought I gained what I forever lost,
They proved to me how I've been losing all along

Times we may haven't know each other as much;
Times were the idea of us had a potential awaiting

W/O

And without my texts, our friendship isn't there,
Without my calls, about them, I won't much know

Without me checking up on them,
I bet on me they would never do

Without my constant efforts of keeping a
connection alive,
Without the one-sided love and appreciation
for them I deeply have,
They would do nothing watching it all fall apart

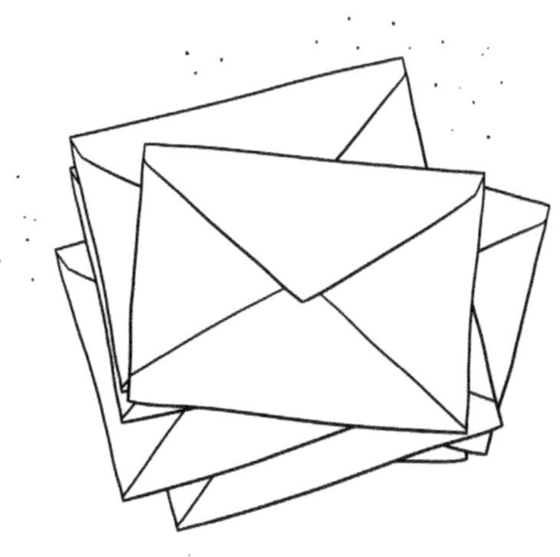

Scars Heal, Bones Mend

Remembering me they never care to,
Away they drift, with no valid reason to

Been the best I ever could for people
I so much loved,
And yet they barely have it within them
acknowledged

Taking my pureness of soul for granted they
always do,
Absorbing the goodness off me until I am
entirely blue

Like swords, their words through my heart hit
Like deserts, draining and tiring their drought is

Me staying forever, they probably assume
and think,
And eventually I will move on, cutting off
every link

Every link that sweet started but bitter ended
Every link that wasn't a cure but a toxic dose

And as time passes, scars heal,
and bones mend,
And happiness blooms, with
no forces of pretend

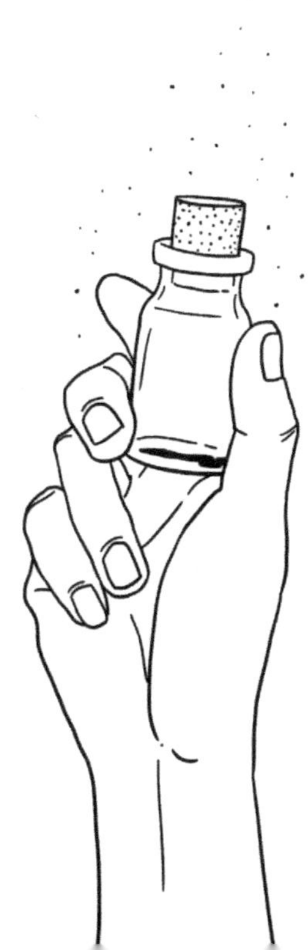

Poison

And when I thought you'd be the one,
Who truly understands the person I am

You didn't, but through you I actually knew,
That even about myself, I didn't much know

My pros you viewed some as cons.
Why? About that I still don't know

Being a friend too good was apparently bad,
And being bad is your way of good somehow

Sticking around regardless, I did all of that endure,
But then leaked your poison, one with no cure

Warned I was, I supposedly had to as fast run,
I didn't though; in a change in you I did believe

Am I right? Or should I have acted differently?
I worry the price I have to pay consequently

Incandescent

Incandescent was the bond between us, forming,
With traits and lots of what we have in common

Changed was my perspective of life meeting you, realizing
There's still good that about, I never knew

Perfect were the moments spent with you around,
Having my true self inadvertently shining out there

A good friend, you made me feel seen.
And to your talks, I'm a listener so keen

The tiny gestures, you so much appreciate,
Surprisingly, people before you never did

Haven't really known you since
much, but yet,
Long-time friends is what they'd
about us bet

Grateful is me having your
friendship in my life,
Without you, I would've been
 in a state so dark

Perfect Pal

Back then I was feeling lost and all alone
In a crowded room I was, still on my own

That's when I met a friend so rare and true
You shone and lit up the room and so I knew

Our conversations and talks makes me feel
so complete
Incandescent our bond is, growing every
time we meet

Our personalities click, our interests too
It's just so fulfilling, being around you

Grateful I am, to be blessed by something real
we share
So superior it is, none other can be on par
nor compare

CHAPTER II:

Comedowns

Passing By

About who we are, they don't really know,
Acquaintances we are to them, or perhaps,
Some random strangers we are, passing by

Background actors we are
In the major films they star

Lucky we would be in their life, to cameo
Or to have some cascading effect on them
somehow

And to be remembered by more than just a
recognizable face
To be remembered by more than just a cool
outfit or a unique name

To be a sweet incident that makes their day
To be a bright memory in their mind engraved

To be the source of laughter and joy,
one we've always longed for
Masking a crumbling state of mind,
which about, they don't really know

Screaming Color

All of a sudden you did have it blissfully ignited
A luminescent bond that had us together united

Skeptical of that I was, and I somehow doubted
How real it was, and if I was able to requite it

Shades of grayscale blasted into pigments
of screaming color
The vibrance was off the charts till it found
its way into becoming duller

Your words, framed a picture candescently
green, and yet,
Your silence, was a thousand swords,
having my heart ripped

Ended once it made its way around a sun,
but still
Remembering the best friend of 365 days,
I always will

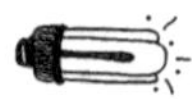

Grayscale

Into grayscale I was fading, until you I had met
and knew
Within me erupted a bright hue, of red, green,
and blue

Your personality complemented mine perfectly,
And your energy just lighted my soul every time

And all I felt with you was a pure rush of serotonin.
Spiraling I was, and in a pit of joy I felt thrown in

Until you were not, you were the one person
I spent a lifetime looking for,
And regardless, I still cherish a friendship that
felt like forever someday

Paths Crossed

And no matter how pure one's soul can be,
Contempt does find its way in some degree

And it breaks even more to lose a real friend,
To lose someone, who about you much knew

Even without conflicts or tense conversations,
Distance affects even the sincerest relations

Ones which one wishes would forever last,
Ones whose worth can never be replaced

To the people I befriended and eventually lost,
To our memories that I have never away tossed,
I pray we'll once again have our paths crossed

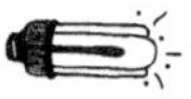

Talk!

Calling me from across the apartment,
they do
Ranting about how I don't talk as much as
I used to

And I keep telling them they just think I don't
Because not much time with them I now spend

But the truth is, my openness is purposely
closed shut
And if I speak my truth, as a son they would
me cut

Because all they want to know is how gracious
and thankful I deeply for them feel,
But never the nightmares of losing them that
every night does part of my heart peel

And all they want to see is my supposed constant
state of happiness,
But never how I go to sleep with nothing but
overwhelming hollowness

And don't I dare speak to them my true emotions
I'd presumably be psychotic, throwing tantrums
and explosions

Sonder

Before I was born, my mom was a carefree
young girl,
Playing with dolls, and having big dreams of
a life not necessarily centered on our own

Before I was born, my dad was an ambitious
young boy,
Looking up to his father the same way I look
up to my own

And eventually, my sister grows into a smart
young lady,
Crafting a life of her own that won't intersect
with mine as much anymore

And as I grow up, I find myself turning
into a wandering young man,
Accomplishing stuff and reaching places
he never thought he ever would

No Moon

Wandering my eyes were, through the skies
high above
Looking for the glorious entity of a moon shining

Yet behind layered curtains of opaque black
that entity hid
Lacking adornment, stood still with emptiness
these skies did

No stars covering up, no constellations distracting
In the blackness, roared loud screams of silence

And so they have faded into a life
diverging off mine
And so hollowness creeps into me,
it's the knowing-them fine

Purpose has from me disintegrated,
like these empty skies with no moon
Singularly keeping me alive still, is a
converging point in our lives yet again

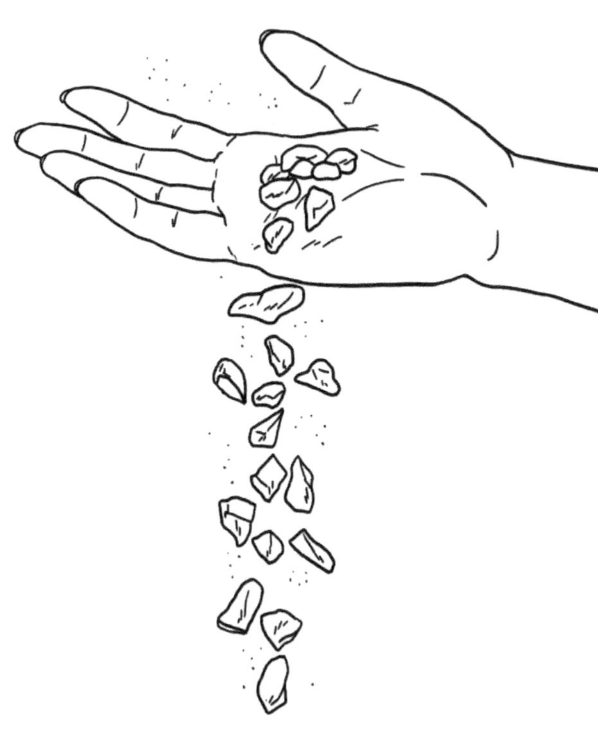

December 10th

Days could've been bad but as worse as
December 10th they could've never been,
The day that had me drowned within the
pain of buried feelings and thoughts

From deep down they resurfaced as a raging flood,
Damaging me like they're coming for blood

Thought I stood a chance, but I've miserably lost,
And within breakdowns, I saw myself falling apart

Those haunting feelings I put down into words,
thinking I was going to get of them rid,
Yet a momentary relief was accompanied by the
overthinking of what I previously did

Heavy my heart was. Sick to the stomach I felt.
No matter how I survive it, I don't think about
this day I'll ever forget

Come & Go

Within the shallowness of who they are, I try to
dive,
With false hopes of having something real thrive

False hopes that a compensation does me await,
For all the energy that from me have eventually
drained

With the care I have given to people but never
received,
With the glamorous first impressions that had
 me deceived

Damaging these experiences were,
but I eventually knew,
People come and go, and rarely they
in one's life stay

Took Root

Took root in me was insurmountable pain
and ever-lasting grief
From a lovely never-lasting phase of my life
that was rather brief

Took root in mind were memories and
incandescent moments that I will forever cherish
And I was fully aware as they formed and faded,
and in real-time, I saw them perish

Took root in heart was an excruciating stance
of letting go and moving on
From an apparent significant other that was
nothing but a sweet con

Took root in mind were saddening senses
of anger and vengeance
From so-called friends who broke my trust
with no shame or repentance

Took root in me was an epiphany
of being acceptant
That I am better off alone,
full-on independent.

CHAPTER III:

Mirror Reflections

Unexpectedly Expected

A deep, complex labyrinth it really is
With no means of escape there is

You're lost the moment you enter
It's a maze so malicious and cruel

Jumped you are whenever a path is taken
And no rules there are, yet no right choice

Expected you are to survive and learn
Yet it makes sure all you face is torture

And so does the unexpected happens always,
Until you eventually know what to expect

No Exit There Is

No exit from this place there is
It makes sure you never find one

And saddening it is to you, being right here
While people are out there, enjoying fancy places

Glad you are there's someone else in here with you
Sorry you are for them to experience that with you

And while they assume it's a source of power,
Nothing this place does but drain you out of it

Put to Pause

A distracting track of sound, your dreams are
put to pause
To focus on the silence of your mind,
the hollowness of your soul

Passion did away vanish and flee,
And enthusiasm was the last green leaf falling
off your tree

Meaningless you sense your existence now is,
And your days are monotone, with nothing new

The missions you ought.
The dreams you once sought.
The ambitions along the journey you
captured and caught.
Memories they are now,
and away they sail in a wrecked boat.

Wrecked by your abandonment.
By feelings of agony and torment.

Not in fault you are, but a need is there
for you to get up and heal
Resuming a track of dreams, one you've
been always meant to hear

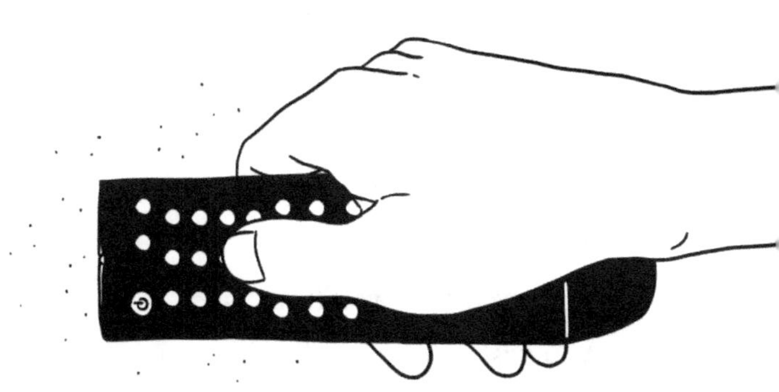

Tunnel

The heavy, painful breath you deeply intake,
The gray, cloudy skies that grow and overtake

Haunting you are flashbacks of joyful days,
Ones that ended, but you still hope would
come back again

A dark, narrow tunnel is where you are stuck in,
And as fast as you can, fiercely, you are running

Seeking an exit, and the light,
Awaiting you on the other side

Happiness, a glowing existence,
will always remain,
And eventually you'll get, what
you wish to obtain

Toxicity

No pain cuts more to the bone than to feel
alone in every crowd,
To feel out of place no matter who you meet
and where you go

To feel like a burden on your friends and
whoever you love,
And to feel so low while everything you need
flies high above

To have your feelings so disregarded,
And to have your presence uncared for

To let go of who makes you enjoy much of
life's simplicity,
Because eventually, you'll have them festered
with much toxicity

Crowded Room

In a crowded room, around them, here you are
Around too many people, yet feeling alone

You look around, but of them,
you recognize none
They call your name, apparently you are known

A lot in common you do have,
you realize and figure
And estrangement fades, into a comfort zone

Between them, you experience
joy you never did before
Your bond has now grown and further shone

In a crowded room, among them, here you are

As They Used To

Even though, you couldn't step back and let them go,
They were the one in whom a true friend you
finally saw

Not so much about each other you now know.
They grew apart too quick for you to anticipate

Cold and dry as the Arctic they now are,
Yet in your head, they were one bright star

Obvious was the contempt that from them sprouted,
You're there always, yet they don't seem to much care

Part of you cannot really hate them no matter
what they do,
They just don't mean to you as much as they used to

Back to When

Back to when you thought in them was a
much needed friend
Back to when you thought what you had
in common would you both bond

Found a decent person in them,
and here you stayed
Yet they were from something so precious blind

And it hurt to be around a person who a lot
in common you have
Yet a burden you feel you are when they
roughly respond

And you kept on trying, and allowing time
for other chances to come
Yet nothing ever progressed and hopes
to continue came to an end

Moved on you did, and other decent people
you will get to befriend
And the greatest friend they have ever wasted
is who you will always remain

Care Less

Too soon it was when it all vanished.
Who they really are wasn't one you can handle

Evergreen forests you once were in,
have utterly dried,
Surviving their drought you could not,
even though you tried

Thirsty enough you were for some recognition,
And not just a person barely to them visible

About them now you
couldn't care less.
Yet before you used to
love them more

Silent Revenge

Pierced, your heart was with their pointed words
Drained, your soul was from their constant rage

A reality you can't avoid
A nightmare you can't flee

Empty, your battery is to them face
Exhausted, you are to even debate

The power to fight is nonexistent
The will to survive is yet to be found

Thoughtful, you are of a meticulous plan
Aware, you are of what the future beholds

A raging revenge does your heart consume, yet
An act of the future does the job for you instead

Their Loss, It Was

Later they'll realize they lost a rare, true gem,
Too bad you'd be moving on from them

You wouldn't have minded to give more and
even pour,
To be a companion, a friend, and a comfort zone

If they would've just appreciated and loved you so,
You could've had something real that'd
forever grow

Their loss though, and never yours,
That, regularly in mind, you need to keep

Catastrophe

Sensors, and smoke detectors
In a home, ensuring it's somewhere safe

You're away, and yet to it connected
In case of an emergency, you're alerted

Yet the alert comes with no action
Corresponding only to your reaction

What if, you noticed late? What if, you didn't see?
A catastrophe would occur, one you can't flee

And so people drop hints and some clues
Hoping you'd figure their emotional cues

To save them from thoughts that had
them drowned
To aid them battle the anxiety their mind
eventually crowned

Not a savior you are, but yet
It's a kind act you'd never regret

Dominoes

From the mistakes of the past and present you learn,
From the experiences, and the tears of joy and pain

You wonder, without them,
who would you be today?
A version of you better?
Or one causing great dismay?

The moments you have cherished,
And others you have totally cursed,
Shaped the person you are today

And like pieces of dominoes they perfectly fall,
Setting you a never-better future, once and for all

Second-Best

An A- for a letter grade
A runner-up for a position

Not someone's go-to friend
Not the favorite of two children

And yet about that, you don't really care or mind
And for others, a lot of happiness you deeply find

The summit you once topped has now collapsed
and harshly fell
And climbing another requires a new story from
you to craft and tell

Unbothered you are as they work hard being first
Because minimal effort still has you second-best

RUNNER-UP!
RUNNER-UP!
RUNNER-UP!
RUNNER-UP!
ER-UP!
RUNNER-UP!
RUNNER-UP!

False Eternity

He was her light that shone bright in the dark,
Incandescent, igniting her spirit and leaving a mark

She saw eternity within his ocean blue eyes,
Of love that would forever last and never die

"Forever" is a word that has its way of deceiving,
A con it is, and a promise never worth believing

For the pain of loss and heartbreak it brings,
Too much it is to bear, too heavy it is to swing

Lived and learned she has, but never again,
Will her heart feel love, or cause it to begin

Now she sees it clearly, it wasn't meant to be
Eternity she once believed in was just a fantasy

Fragile

And the love that once brought her profound joy,
Is now flickers of memories, perhaps just a ploy

A sanctuary it was from the pain and heartbreak
of the past,
A love it was that made her heart skip and
beat fast

In a crowded room, their secret moments did
her embrace,
And together they shared a love that once wasn't
to ever cease

For love is a fragile thing that's ultimately broken,
And hearts can be shattered by what's left
unspoken

She thought this love she had would never end,
But destiny had its own saddening trend

Another Time, Another Space

In another time, in even another space
Finding the right friends and a soulmate for
life wouldn't be as hard to chase

An armor one puts when they're out to the world
Wouldn't be an obstacle from having their true
personality to other people sold

Awkwardness would throw itself out of the
highest window
Its minor presence and its moments can still
be of a win though

Bonding over fun interests would be as seamless
and instant
And one wouldn't worry about shallow talks
that grows people distant

In another time, in another space even
One throws away the self-doubts they now
heavily believe in

Serenity

Serenity is something he'll never find
As chaos stirs, blurs, and fills his mind

Just like following a detour leading to an
abrupt ending
And nothing is beyond that except a decision
pending

Serenity in relationships he'll never get
Never felt appreciated for who he is yet

And he's twenty-one writing words of poetry
in a dorm room
Missing home, his family, and overusing his
dad's perfume

Serenity is only there when he's present
with his sister
Fear goes away, even when they are to face
what's sinister

Serenity fades away in every other
environment and situation
Surviving through a profound mess by
some means of commutation

Only Once

Coming in and out they are about
A crowd bonded by a single route

Of each's background they are mostly naive
Joined by silence and noise until they leave

To work, to home, to some fun space they
are headed
Different purposes, thoughts, and beliefs in
here embedded

And only once they may in this life into
each other run
Only in this moment they are experiencing
until it's gone

Bejeweled

Real, yet it felt like a fever dream
A night like no other, an unforgettable gleam

Melodies floated, magic spread in the air
Weaving together, into a moment so rare

The stage bejeweled, a celestial sight
Transcending time, a shared delight

Voices soared, hearts were intertwined
And nothing but fun, in this venue we find

Breathless, in awe, souls
incandescent
An experience, in memory,
forever present

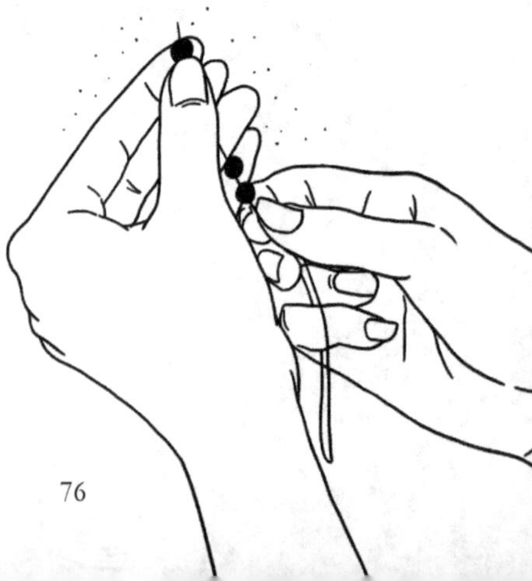

Epilogue

Writing Incandescent, I channeled the emotions felt through various relationships, ones I have personally experienced and others I have observed and have left me deeply thinking. We all experience relationships with nuances of different shades: ones that miserably failed, ones that were draining, ones that were fun as long as they lasted, and ones that seem to last for a life-time.

What struck me a lot and still does is this one type of connection: friendship. No type of human connection is ever as precious as real friendship, where aside from everything and the differences you might have you just click together for what you have in common, or may be because simply you have found in each other a soul that understands you and accepts you for who you truly are, your good and bad, both equally.

Real friends will light up your soul, their presence will aid healing your wounds, and their spirit will complement yours perfectly.

Sometimes they are just not like that, and you feel like giving more than what you receive; it happens. Most effectively, a remedy for that would be for you to drift away and eventually move on, but let's be frank, sometimes we just cannot do that, and we end up enduring toxicity to be surrounded by people who we can have fun moments with.

No matter how alone you feel right now, you will find your true people and friends someday. Maybe in days, months, or even years, but eventually you will, I promise you that.

www.ingramcontent.com/pod-product-compliance
Lightning Source LLC
Chambersburg PA
CBHW051004050726

47592CB00007B/2701